ABSOLUTE BEGINNERS
Banjo

T0080292

Project Editors: Heather Ramage and Rachel L. Conrad.
Photography: Geoff Green.

Photos on page 6 by and courtesy of Stan Jay/Mandolin Bros.
Electric Banjo is a Deering Crossfire
Open Back Banjo is a Vega Tubaphone (dated 1924)

Interior design and layout: Len Vogler.

ISBN 978-0-8256-3499-4

Visit Hal Leonard Online at
www.halleonard.com

Contact us:
Hal Leonard
7777 West Bluemound Road
Milwaukee, WI 53213
Email: info@halleonard.com

In Europe, contact:
Hal Leonard Europe Limited
42 Wigmore Street
Marylebone, London, W1U 2RN
Email: info@halleonardeurope.com

In Australia, contact:
Hal Leonard Australia Pty. Ltd.
4 Lentara Court
Cheltenham, Victoria, 3192 Australia
Email: info@halleonard.com.au

Table of Contents

4 Online Audio Track Listing

Track 1: G tuning

Track 2: G chord

Track 3: D7 chord

Track 4: Alternating G and D7 chords

Track 5: C chord

Track 6: Alternating G and C chord

Track 7: Skip To My Lou with strumming

Track 8: Man Of Constant Sorrow with strumming

Track 9: Will The Circle Be Unbroken with strumming

Track 10: Long Journey Home with strumming

Track 11: Picking with the right hand

Track 12: Alternating-thumb roll demonstration

Track 13: Skip To My Lou with alternating-thumb roll

Track 14: G, C, and D7 chords with alternating-thumb roll

Track 15: Forward-backward roll demonstration

Track 16: G, C, and D7 chords with forward-backward roll

Track 17: Man Of Constant Sorrow with forward-backward roll

Track 18: Will The Circle Be Unbroken with alternating-thumb roll

Track 19: Long Journey Home with alternating-thumb roll

Track 20: Will The Circle Be Unbroken with forward-backward roll

Track 21: Long Journey Home with forward-backward roll

Track 22: Alternating-thumb and forward-backward rolls for G, C, and D7 chord

Track 23: Will The Circle Be Unbroken with alternating-thumb and forward-backward rolls

Track 24: Long Journey Home with alternating-thumb and forward-backward rolls

Track 25: G, C, and D7 chords with pinch pattern

Track 26: Skip To My Lou with pinch pattern

Track 27: Man Of Constant Sorrow with pinch pattern

Track 28: Will The Circle Be Unbroken with pinch pattern

Track 29: Long Journey Home with pinch pattern

Track 30: Skip To My Lou with alternating-thumb roll and pinch pattern

Track 31: Skip To My Lou with forward-backward roll and pinch pattern

Track 32: Skip To My Lou easy melody

Track 33: Skip To My Lou easy melody with band accompaniment

Track 34: Skip To My Lou melody using alternating-thumb roll and pinch pattern

Track 35: Skip To My Lou melody with band accompaniment

Track 36: Skip To My Lou melody with forward-backward roll and pinch pattern

Track 37: Skip To My Lou melody with band accompaniment

Track 38: Skip To My Lou with band accompaniment, no banjo

Track 39: Man Of Constant Sorrow with band accompaniment, no banjo

Track 40: Will The Circle Be Unbroken with band accompaniment, no banjo

Track 41: Long Journey Home with band accompaniment, no banjo

Track 42: Cripple Creek demonstration

Track 43: Cripple Creek with band accompaniment

Track 44: Cripple Creek with band accompaniment, no banjo

Welcome to *Absolute Beginners Banjo*! These days, the banjo is used not only in bluegrass, country, and folk music, but is also heard more frequently in jazz, rock, and classical music. This book gets you started in the right direction by guiding you from the very first time you take your banjo out of its case to playing your first songs.

Easy-to-follow instructions will guide you through:
Learning the parts of your banjo
Changing strings on your banjo
Holding and tuning your banjo
Fretting chords
Placing picks on your right hand
Playing your first roll patterns
Playing your first songs

Learning how to play the banjo is fun but challenging. Don't forget to listen and play along with the accompanying audio. This will speed your progress and give you confidence that you're getting the correct sounds from your banjo.

In this book, we will focus on learning the basics of bluegrass banjo, the most widely played banjo style in the world today. However, you can use these same techniques to play other kinds of music as well. At the end of this book, you'll find recommendations to help you continue your musical journey with the banjo.

Practicing Tips

Every good player has spent many hours practicing. Set a personal practice schedule and try your best to stick to it. Twenty minutes of playing each day is better than cramming several hours in on the weekend (but that's better than no practice at all!). Also, take things one step at a time and be patient with your progress. It takes a while for your brain and fingers to become comfortable with these new skills.

Making the most of your practice time

1. Find time to practice every day, even if it's just for a short period of time. If you're able, keep the banjo out of its case and ready to play for a few minutes at any time (but make sure that it's in a safe location).

2. Spend most of your practice time working specifically on the new techniques that you're trying to master. If you have time at the end of each session, review pieces you already know to keep them in your memory.

3. Learn to play with a metronome. There are also several computer programs that allow you to vary the tempo of recordings so that you can play along with your favorite songs at the speed that works best for you. Try one of these to see if it makes your practice more fun.

4. Set realistic short, medium, and long-range goals but don't be afraid to adjust them. Make sure that what you practice helps you achieve these goals.

5. Learn one thing at a time and learn it well before moving on to the next technique or tune.

6. It usually takes a number of months before even the most talented banjo player can play with speed and power. Strive for a clear tone and good volume before worrying about speed.

7. Be patient! Bluegrass banjo is a highly virtuosic art form that takes time to learn well. Keep playing and you'll reach your goals.

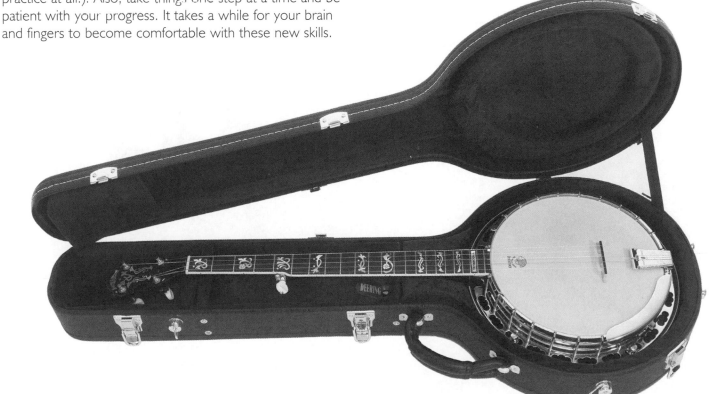

Types of 5-String Banjos

The five-string banjo has one string that is shorter than the others. The tuning peg for this string is located almost halfway up the neck. While different kinds of five-string banjos are associated with different styles of music, all of these instruments can be tuned and played in the same way. It is possible to play any kind of banjo music on any type of banjo.

A resonator banjo has a shallow, bowl-shaped chamber that is attached to the main body of the instrument. This is the kind of banjo that is usually used in bluegrass music.

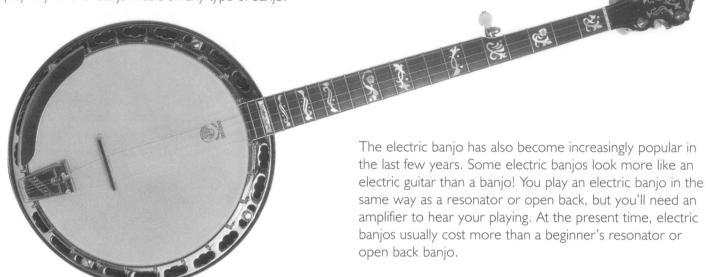

Resonator Banjo

The electric banjo has also become increasingly popular in the last few years. Some electric banjos look more like an electric guitar than a banjo! You play an electric banjo in the same way as a resonator or open back, but you'll need an amplifier to hear your playing. At the present time, electric banjos usually cost more than a beginner's resonator or open back banjo.

An open back banjo enables you to see the inside of the banjo from the back of the instrument. This kind of banjo lacks a resonator and is usually used in folk and old-time music.

Resonator banjos tend to be louder, while open back banjos are usually lighter in weight and are sometimes cheaper in price. In most other aspects, these two kinds of banjos are almost identical.

Open Back Banjo

Electric Banjo

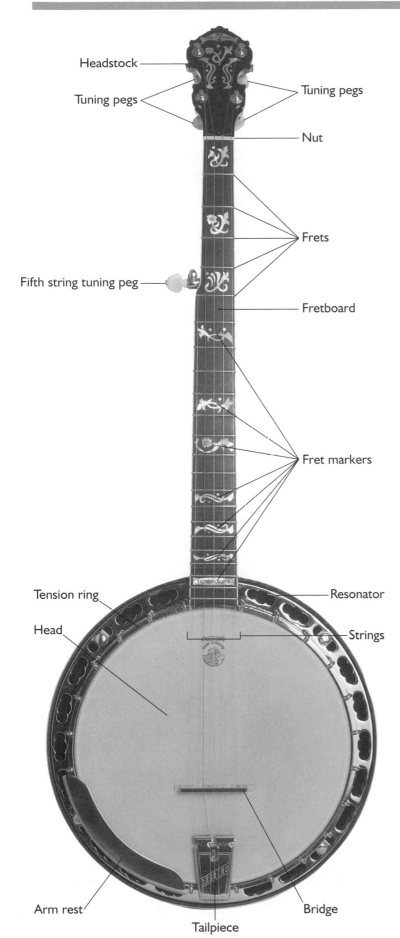

Headstock

Tuning pegs

Tuning pegs

Nut

Frets

Fifth string tuning peg

Fretboard

Fret markers

Tension ring

Resonator

Head

Strings

Arm rest

Bridge

Tailpiece

The *headstock* has four *tuning pegs*, two on each side. The strings are threaded to the inside of each tuning peg and guided into a corresponding slot on the *nut*. Each string has a number name as well as a note name. The fifth string is located five frets up the neck and has a separate tuning peg.

The strings travel up the *fretboard* across the *frets* of the banjo neck. As a string is fretted, its length becomes shorter and its pitch becomes higher. The first fret is located just on the other side of the nut from the headstock. The second fret is the next highest fret and the third fret is beyond that, all the way up to the twenty-second fret. *Fret markers* are positioned on the fretboard to help you see where you are on the neck.

There are often dots on the side of the neck that correspond to your fret markers. These dots help you to see where you are without having to look directly at the fretboard.

The strings extend over the plastic *head* of the banjo and are guided through a corresponding slot at the *bridge*. On most banjos, the bridge is moveable and has a standard optimal position that allows the fretted notes to stay in tune. The correct position of the bridge is a bit different for each banjo and should come properly set upon purchase.

The tension of the banjo head can be adjusted by tightening or loosening the brackets with a banjo wrench. If you have a banjo with a *resonator*, you'll need to remove the resonator to adjust the head tension.

The tension of the banjo head affects the sound production of the instrument, specifically the volume, tone quality, and the intonation. A properly tightened banjo head will produce a clear, crisp tone and hold its intonation. When not properly adjusted, the instrument will produce a dull, unfocused sound, lose volume, and will go out of tune more easily.

You will want to find the middle ground that produces the best sound from your instrument. Be sure not to over-tighten the banjo head, as over-tightening may cause damage to the body of the instrument.

The strings are held at the bottom of the banjo by the *tailpiece*. There are several different types of tailpieces, each with a slightly different way of holding the string.

> **TIP**
> Keep your banjo away from extremes of heat and cold. It is a good idea to take the banjo to a music store that specializes in acoustic instruments for periodic checkups and adjustments.

Strings and Things

When it becomes difficult to tune the banjo or if the strings show signs of obvious wear, it's a good idea to replace them. Strings are packaged in sets and are labeled as light, medium-light, or medium according to the thickness of the diameter of each string (which is measured in 1/1000's of an inch). Each string is numbered first through fifth to indicate where it is placed on the banjo. Experiment with different sets to see which you like best.

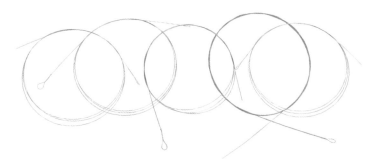

Replace each string one at a time. Take note of how the old string is attached before removing it. You can leave the other strings up to pitch while you are changing a string. Most banjos use loop end strings. Attach the looped end at the tailpiece.

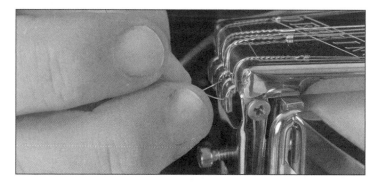

Place the string in the appropriate *notch* in the bridge and tailpiece and through the hole in the shaft of the appropriate tuning peg. Don't forget to thread the string from the inside of the tuning shaft for strings one through four.

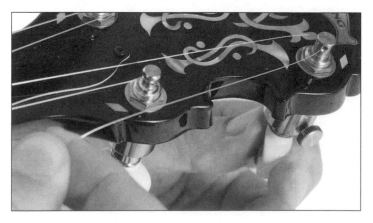

Pull most of the excess string length through the hole so that you only need to wind the string around the shaft three or four times. It's a good idea to pin the excess part of the string against the shaft as it is brought up to tension. This prevents the excess string from slipping back through the hole and causing the string to lose tension and go out of tune.

Tune the strings by turning the tuning pegs. By increasing tension on the string, its sound (or *pitch*) becomes higher. By decreasing tension, the pitch becomes lower. Turn the fourth and third string pegs counterclockwise to raise the pitch of the string, and clockwise to lower the pitch. Turn the second and first strings clockwise to raise the pitch and counterclockwise to lower the pitch.

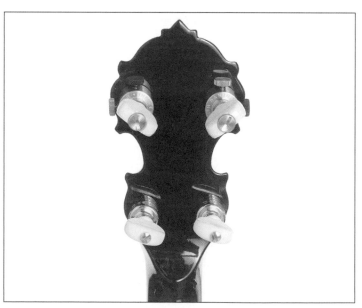

For most banjos, turning the fifth string peg counter-clockwise will raise the pitch while turning clockwise will lower the pitch. When the string is tuned to the desired pitch, clip off the excess with wire cutters.

TIP
New strings often take a day or two to settle in. Your banjo will require extra tuning during this break-in period.

You will most likely sit down for practicing at home. However, you may prefer to stand when playing with others in a jam session. Sitting or standing, it is a good idea to use a strap to balance your banjo and to keep both hands free for playing.

It is best to use an actual banjo strap rather than a guitar strap. A banjo strap should be adjustable in length and will have hooks or some other kind of attachment on both ends of the strap. To attach, fit the strap hooks through the brackets on the banjo *pot*, or body of the instrument.

To provide optimum support, it is best to attach one end of the strap to a bracket underneath the tailpiece. Extend the strap under your right arm, up and across your back and over your left shoulder.

Attach the other end of the strap to a bracket below the neck. Experiment with different lengths of the strap to see what feels right to you. Keep in mind that your left hand should not be supporting the weight of the neck—it's the strap's job to keep the banjo balanced and the neck upright.

Position the neck so that the headstock isn't above eye level or below a horizontal position.

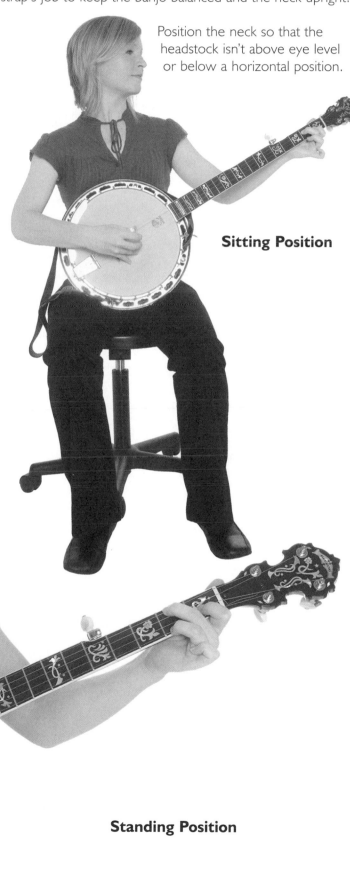

Sitting Position

Standing Position

There are many different tunings used by banjo players but the most common tuning is known as *G tuning*. The five pitches in this tuning correspond to the notes that make up a G chord. (A *chord* is three or more notes played together.)

Don't forget that the short fifth string is the highest-pitched string on the banjo and the fourth string is the lowest. This is unique to the banjo and is a remnant of its African ancestry. Here are the notes of G tuning beginning with the lowest pitch on the fourth string and going up to the highest pitch on the fifth string, demonstrated by **Track 1** 🔊 on the accompanying audio. (Tune your banjo to the recording so that you can play along in tune with the backing tracks.)

Fourth string = D	(lowest pitch)
Third string = G	↑
Second string = B	
First string = D	↓
Fifth string = G	(highest pitch)

Note that both the fourth and first strings are tuned to a D note and both the third and fifth strings are tuned to a G note. The first-string D pitch is an *octave* (eight pitches) higher than the fourth-string D and the fifth-string G is an octave higher than the third-string G pitch.

There are several different ways to tune the banjo. You can tune it by using a pitch pipe or an electronic tuner. You can also tune the banjo to itself using one of its strings as a guide, or you can tune your banjo to another instrument such as a piano, guitar, or another banjo.

Relative Tuning

If one of your strings is in tune, you can tune the rest of your banjo to that string. This is called *relative tuning* because you are tuning the banjo to itself, not to an outside source. Follow the diagram below to tune your banjo in this way.

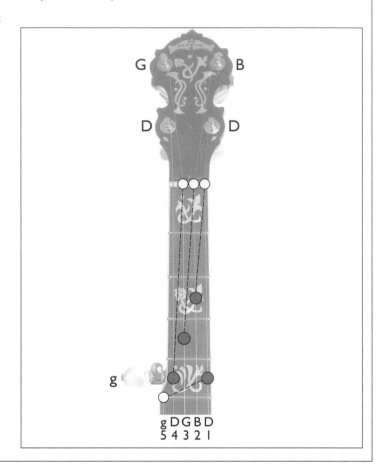

g D G B D
5 4 3 2 1

Using an Electronic Tuner

An electronic tuner is a great and inexpensive accessory to help you tune. Some tuners have a built-in microphone while others clip directly onto the headstock of your banjo.

Most tuners have a moving needle or LED indicator that lets you know whether a string is too high (or *sharp*) or too low (or *flat*). When using an electronic tuner, strike the note you want to tune and read the tuner's result, adjusting the string up or down in tension as needed. If the string is significantly higher or lower than the desired pitch, the tuner will give you the letter name of the note that the string is closest to in pitch.

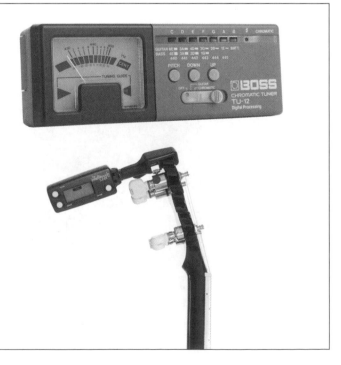

Tuning to Other Instruments

You can get one or more strings in tune by using another instrument as a guide and then tune the rest of your banjo using the relative tuning process just described.

The fourth, third, and second strings of your banjo are tuned to the same pitches as the fourth, third, and second strings on the guitar (D, G, and B). If you're playing with a piano, the third string of the banjo is the G note that is found below Middle C on the piano.

Tuning the banjo to a guitar

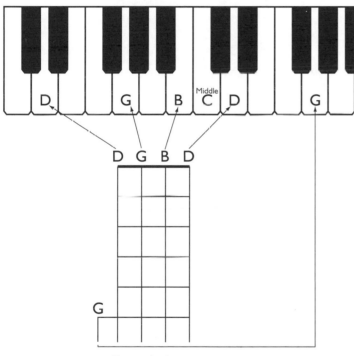

Tuning the banjo to a piano

Checkpoint
What you've learned so far:
• The names of the parts of the banjo
• How to comfortably hold the banjo
• How to change strings
• The different ways to tune a banjo

Left-Hand Position

The first skill you'll need to learn is how to use your left-hand fingers to fret the strings on the banjo in order to create new notes and chords. It's important to develop a good left-hand position to make fretting easier.

The fretting fingers are numbered 1, 2, 3, and 4, and correspond to the index, middle, ring, and pinky fingers.

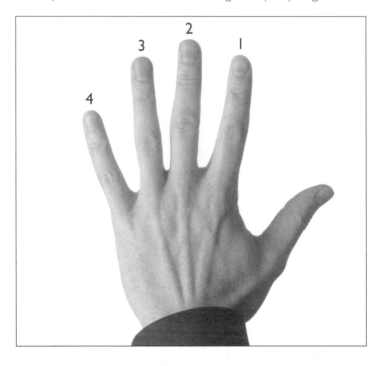

Keeping the wrist relaxed and straight, place the left-hand thumb on the upper part of the back of the neck opposite the space between the first and second frets. Remember that the left hand shouldn't be supporting the weight of the banjo neck. As you fret, remember to relax your shoulder, arm, and elbow. Depending upon the size of your hand, you may end up cradling the neck between your thumb and fingers or you may touch the bottom part of the banjo neck with the side of your left hand.

Now let's try fretting the third string behind the second fret using the left-hand middle finger. Place the tip of the finger close to the back edge of the fret but not on top of it. Vary the amount of pressure to find how much force you need to get a clear sound, being careful not to apply too much pressure. If you already play guitar, you'll discover that it doesn't take as much strength to get a good fretted string sound on the banjo.

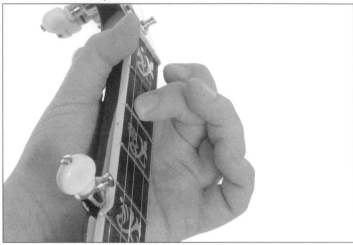

As you fret any string, be careful not to mute the adjacent string with the side of your fretting finger. If this happens, try adjusting your hand position to enable your finger to approach the string from a more vertical position.

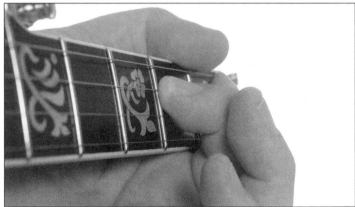

Incorrect finger position

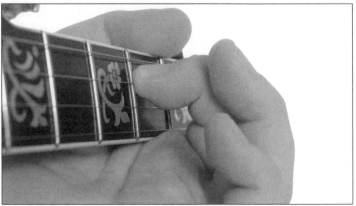

Correct finger position

Chord Diagrams

A *chord diagram* is a widely used method to express which fingers and frets are used to play banjo chords. If you turn the banjo around with the neck facing you, you'll see how the banjo neck is represented in a chord diagram.

The vertical lines represent the banjo strings, with the leftmost line being the fourth string and the rightmost line being the first string. Since it is fretted infrequently, the fifth string is usually not shown in a chord diagram. The thick horizontal line at the top represents the nut. The second line from the top is the first fret and the line below is the second fret. Circles indicate which strings are fretted and at what fret. The numbers inside the circles tell you which fingers are used at each position.

Now let's try fretting a few chords. Chords can be happy or melancholy and they can be simple or complex in their structure. Luckily for banjo players, a good deal of bluegrass, country, and folk music is played with just three chords.

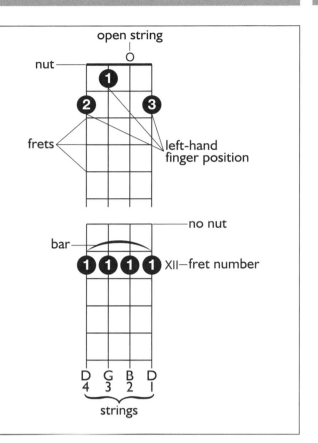

The G Chord

The most important of these chords is the G chord. You don't have to fret anything at all to play this chord because the unfretted (or "open") banjo strings in G tuning already supply all of the notes you need.

Try strumming with your right-hand thumb across all five strings in a downward motion beginning with the fifth string and ending with the first string. If your banjo is properly in tune, you should hear the bright and happy sound of the G major chord.

Track 2 🔊 **G chord**

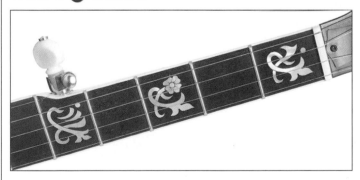

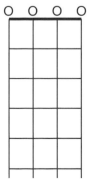

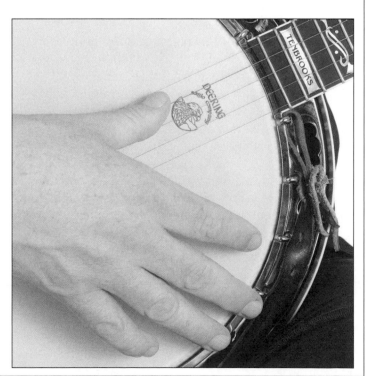

The D7 Chord

Now let's try fretting a D7 chord. This chord is called a *seventh* chord because it contains an additional note not found in a major chord. However, it's an easy chord to fret on the banjo. Place the left-hand middle finger behind the second fret on the third string, and the index finger behind the first fret on the second string.

Track 3 🔊 **D7 chord**

Strum down with your thumb once again across strings 4 through 1 while fretting the D7 chord, making sure that your two fretted notes are ringing clearly and that your left-hand fingers are not touching the adjacent open fourth and first strings.

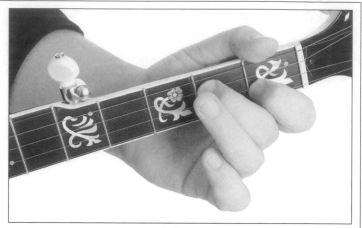

D7

Alternating between G and D7

Now let's try alternating between the G and D7 chords. Since the G chord is played with all open strings, you can prepare for the D7 chord by keeping the two left-hand fingers you use to fret this chord close to the fingerboard, ready to fret at a moment's notice.

Strum a G chord, moving down across all five strings with your thumb. Now fret the D7 chord and strum once again. This time it's okay to strum across all five strings, even though the fifth string is technically not a part of the D7 chord. Listen to the difference in sound between the two chords and also listen to make sure that your D7 chord is sounding clearly, with no string buzzing.

Alternate back and forth between the G and D7 chords with steady strums in the right hand to get used to the idea of moving between these two chords. Remember not to lift your fretting fingers very high off of the fingerboard as you play the G chord.

At first, don't worry about changing chords and strumming quickly. Go as slow as you need to get the best sound possible while fretting the D7 chord. As you continue to practice, you will be able to fret the D7 chord more quickly, at which point you can increase the speed of your right-hand strumming.

Track 4 🔊 **Alternating between G and D7 chords**

G

D7

TIP

Remember that as you strum across the banjo strings with your right-hand thumb, you'll hear the highest-pitched string first and then the lowest-pitched string immediately after that.

The C Chord

Now let's learn another chord that you'll play a lot in all kinds of banjo music: the C chord. This chord uses three left-hand fretting fingers with an open, unfretted third string.

Track 5 🔊 **C chord**

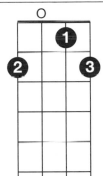

Try to avoid touching the open third string with either the middle or index fingers. You might have to move the left-hand thumb down and bring the left hand forward just a bit to fret the fourth string without touching the third string, as shown below.

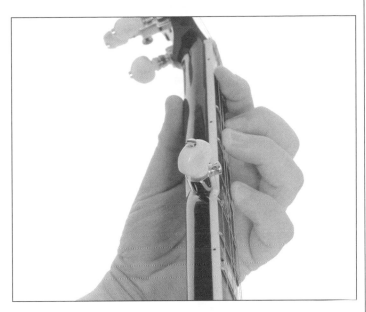

Strum down once again across all five strings with the thumb. Listen to make sure that all fretted strings are ringing clearly and that you can also clearly hear the open third string.

Alternating between G and C

After you are comfortable fretting the C chord by itself, try alternating between the G and C chords with a steady strum in the right hand. As you play the G chord, keep the left-hand fretting fingers just above the fingerboard, ready to fret the C chord.

Place accuracy before speed. As you begin to fret the C chord more easily, try increasing the speed of your right-hand strums.

Track 6 🔊 **Alternating between G and C chords**

TIP

As you fret a chord, try to place all of the left-hand fingers used to make that chord down on the neck in the proper fretting position at the same time. This skill might be difficult at first to master, but with a little practice you'll find that this approach will increase your left-hand speed.

Checkpoint

What you've learned so far:
- Left-hand position for fretting chords
- How to play the G, C, and D7 chords
- Switching between chords while strumming with the right-hand thumb

Let's Play!

Now that you're familiar with the G, C, and D7 chords, let's play some music!

Every song has a *melody* as well as something called a *chord progression*. The melody is that part of the song that you might hum or sing, while the chord progression consists of the chords that go along with the melody. As you learn a chord progression, you become familiar not only with the names of the chords that are used but also how long each chord lasts and in what order they are played.

Many players have trouble at first changing from one chord to another without stopping. However, as you become more comfortable remembering and fretting the chords you need, you will soon be able to change smoothly from one chord to the next while keeping a steady rhythm in the right hand.

Track 7 demonstrates the chord progression and vocal melody to "Skip to My Lou," played slowly. Strum down once for each stroke indicated by a slash, keeping as steady a beat as you can by spacing the strums out evenly in time. (*Barlines* break up the music into *bars* or *measures* and make it easier to count and play in time. More about them later.)

Four metronome clicks occur before the beginning of the song to give you the tempo. Beginning with the fifth click, play along by strumming once for each click, changing chords as indicated above the line. The chord progression is played through three times and features the chorus, a verse, and another chorus (see **Additional Lyrics** on page 38). As you repeat the progression, go straight from the last strum indicated back to the first strum without interrupting the beat.

Skip to My Lou

Track 7

G				D7			
/	/	/	/	/	/	/	/

Skip,   skip,   skip   to   my   Lou.   Skip,   skip,   skip   to   my   Lou.

G				D7		G	*(play three times)*
/	/	/	/	/	/	/	/

Skip,   skip,   skip   to   my   Lou.   Skip   to   my   Lou   my   dar - ling.

TIP

It's not uncommon to lose your place every now and then while playing along with others or with the audio track. When this happens, it's best to stop playing for a moment and join in when you can at any point in the song with strums at the same tempo.

Now let's try a few more bluegrass favorites. You'll learn these tunes faster by playing along with the audio tracks.

The chord progression for "Man of Constant Sorrow" is played through two times and features the first two verses.

MAN OF CONSTANT SORROW

Track 8

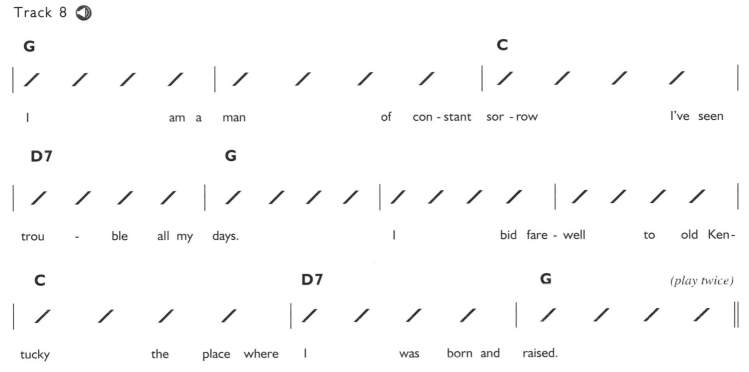

The chord progression for "Will the Circle Be Unbroken" is played two times and features the first verse and chorus of this song.

WILL THE CIRCLE BE UNBROKEN

Track 9

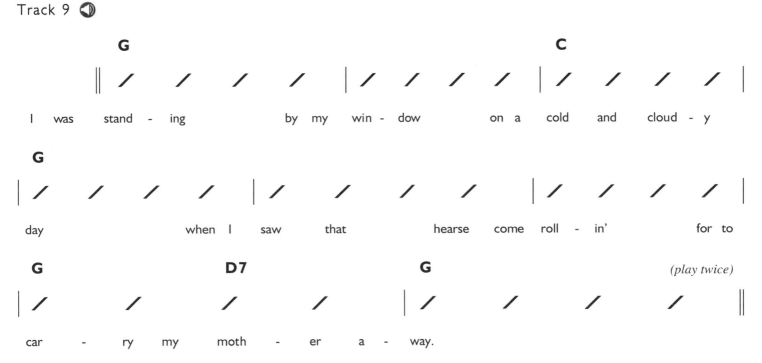

Let's Play!

The chord progression for "Long Journey Home" is played
two times and features the chorus and first verse.

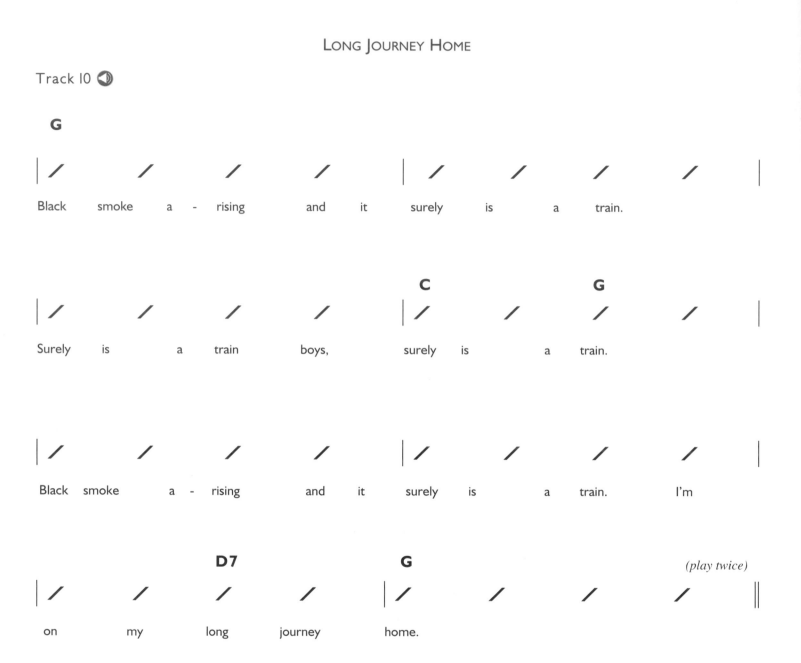

LONG JOURNEY HOME

Track 10

G

Black smoke a - rising and it surely is a train.

C   **G**

Surely is a train boys, surely is a train.

Black smoke a - rising and it surely is a train. I'm

D7   **G**   *(play twice)*

on my long journey home.

TIP
Try to learn the chord progression as quickly as you can so that
you can look at your right or left hand while playing rather than
looking at the pages of this book!

Now it's time to get picks on our right-hand fingers and learn some of the actual playing techniques used by bluegrass banjo players.

Picks

Bluegrass banjo playing is known as a *three-finger picking style*. We use *picks* on the thumb, index, and middle fingers of the right hand in order to get the volume needed to play with others in a jam session or bluegrass band. Most players prefer a plastic *thumbpick* and two metal *fingerpicks*. Note how the picks are placed on the hand.

Select a thumbpick that fits snugly on your thumb. Experiment with different kinds of picks to see what kind works best for you.

You'll have to shape the bands of the metal fingerpicks so that the picks are snug on your fingers. Many players also like to bend the blade of the fingerpick to match the curve at the end of their fingers.

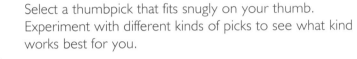

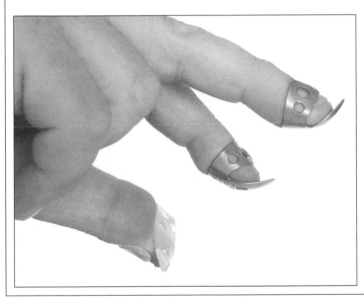
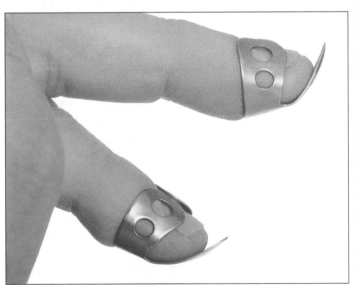
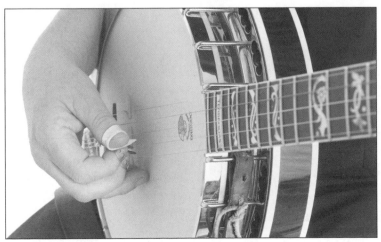

Right-Hand Positioning

Here's a quick way to get your right hand set in a good playing position:

Relax your right arm and hand, letting the arm dangle loosely at the side of your body. Note the position of your right hand. When the hand is relaxed, it should assume a cupped position with all of the finger joints slightly bent.

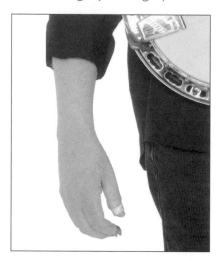

As you maintain this relaxed position, rest the forearm against the armrest or the side of the banjo with the right hand now positioned over and above the banjo strings.

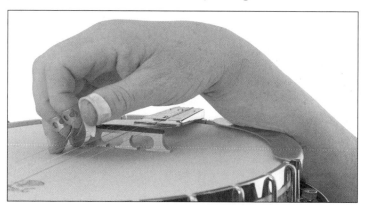

You'll want to anchor the right hand with the ring or pinky finger—or preferably both. To do this, move the forearm back so that the ring and pinky fingers are resting on the head close to the bridge, but not actually touching it.

Your wrist should be arched. Don't let the wrist or forearm touch the banjo head.

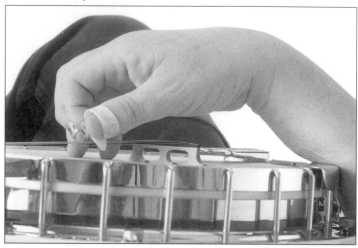

It is important to relax as much as you can while picking with the right hand. In bluegrass-style banjo playing, the thumb (**T**) usually plays the fifth, fourth, third, and second strings, moving downward across the strings. The index (**I**) finger usually plays the third and second strings, and the middle (**M**) finger usually plays the first string. Both of these fingers move upward across the strings.

Track 11 ◖)) demonstrates which right-hand fingers play which strings.

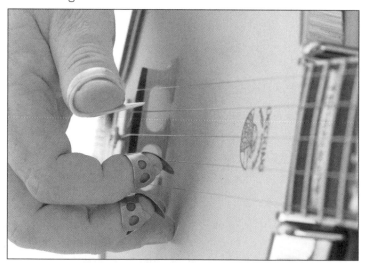

Try playing all of the above string/right-hand finger combinations slowly to hear and feel the sound of the fingerpicks against the strings. Experiment with hand placement to get a better position over the strings and work for a clean and clear sound from the picks.

Right-hand positioning is probably the most challenging aspect of bluegrass banjo playing, so be patient. It will probably take a few weeks of practice to find a right-hand position that feels comfortable for you.

Chord Dictionary

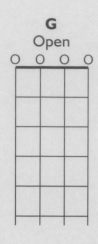

G
Open

G

G
VII

G
XII

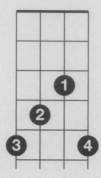

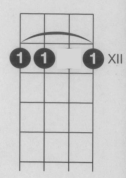

G
XV

C

C

C
VIII

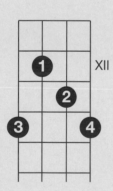

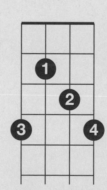

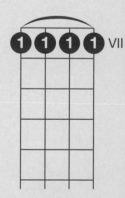

C
XII

D7

D

D
VII

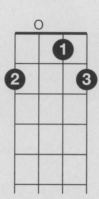

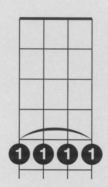

D
X

D
XIV

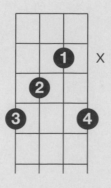

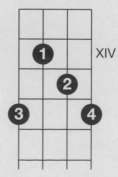

ABSOLUTE BEGINNERS
Banjo

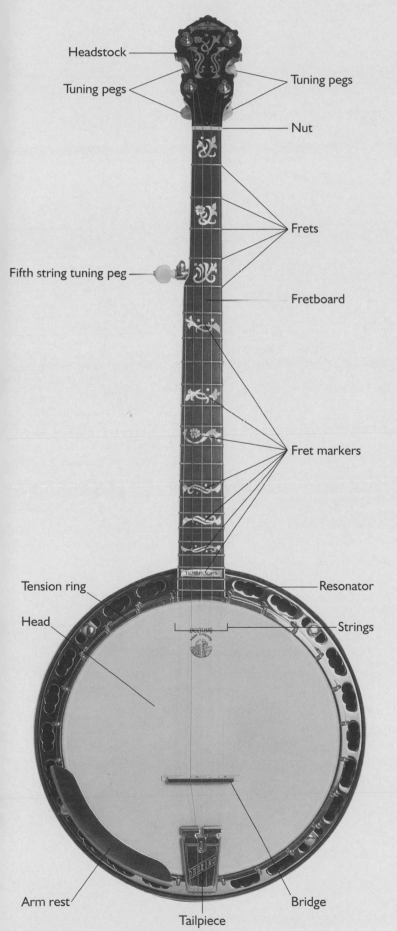

Headstock

Tuning pegs

Tuning pegs

Nut

Frets

Fifth string tuning peg

Fretboard

Fret markers

Tension ring

Head

Resonator

Strings

Arm rest

Bridge

Tailpiece

Parts of the Banjo

The *headstock* has four *tuning pegs*, two on each side. The strings are threaded to the inside of each tuning peg and guided into a corresponding slot on the *nut*. Each string has a number name as well as a note name. The fifth string is located five frets up the neck and has a separate tuning peg.

The strings travel up the *fretboard* across the *frets* of the banjo neck. As a string is fretted, its length becomes shorter and its pitch becomes higher. The first fret is located just on the other side of the nut from the headstock. The second fret is the next highest fret and the third fret is beyond that, all the way up to the twenty-second fret. *Fret markers* are positioned on the fretboard to help you see where you are on the neck.

There are often dots on the side of the neck that correspond to your fret markers. These dots help you to see where you are without having to look directly at the fretboard.

The strings extend over the plastic *head* of the banjo and are guided through a corresponding slot at the *bridge*. On most banjos, the bridge is moveable and has a standard optimal position that allows the fretted notes to stay in tune. The correct position of the bridge is a bit different for each banjo and should come properly set upon purchase.

The tension of the banjo head can be adjusted by tightening or loosening the brackets with a banjo wrench. If you have a banjo with a *resonator*, you'll need to remove the resonator to adjust the head tension.

The tension of the banjo head affects the sound production of the instrument, specifically the volume, tone quality, and the intonation. A properly tightened banjo head will produce a clear, crisp tone and hold its intonation. When not properly adjusted, the instrument will produce a dull, unfocused sound, lose volume, and will go out of tune more easily.

You will want to find the middle ground that produces the best sound from your instrument. Be sure not to over-tighten the banjo head, as over-tightening may cause damage to the body of the instrument.

The strings are held at the bottom of the banjo by the *tailpiece*. There are several different types of tailpieces, each with a slightly different way of holding the string.

Roll patterns are the right-hand note sequences that are an important part of the fast sound of bluegrass banjo playing. We usually don't play the same string or use the same right-hand finger twice in a row in a roll pattern. For the majority of songs that we play, roll patterns will be made up of eight notes of equal length, which we'll call *eighth notes* (because eight of them fit into one measure). Count "1 & 2 & 3 & 4 &" for a full measure of eighth notes. (For more about measures, see **Reading Tablature** on page 23.)

Let's try playing the *alternating-thumb roll* for the G chord. As its name implies, we will be using the right-hand thumb to play every other note in this roll. **T** indicates that the string is played by the right-hand thumb, **I** indicates that the string is played by the right-hand index finger, and **M** indicates that the string is played by the right-hand middle finger. The bottom line indicates the counting that goes along with most roll patterns.

Track 12 🔊 demonstrates the alternating-thumb roll.

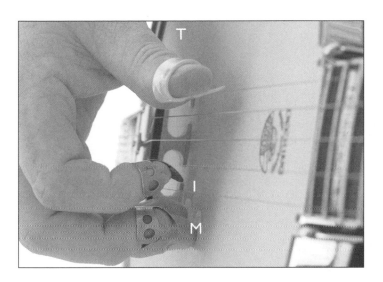

 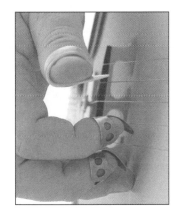  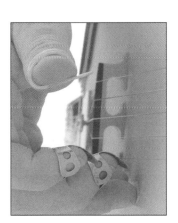

Strings:	3	2	5	I
Right hand:	T	I	T	M
Count:	1	+	2	+

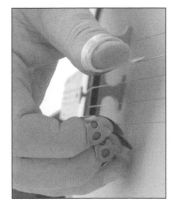   

Strings:	4	2	5	I
Right hand:	T	I	T	M
Count:	3	+	4	+

The Alternating-Thumb Roll

Roll patterns are a great way for the banjo to accompany songs. **Track 13** 🔊 demonstrates the alternating-thumb roll in "Skip to My Lou." This time, you'll hear a count-in to give you the proper tempo and you'll also hear guitar, mandolin, and bass in the accompaniment.

As you play with the track, you will want to play two roll pattern notes for every click that you hear on the recording. Don't worry about singing along with the track—focus on your banjo playing and following the chord progression along with the other musicians in the band.

SKIP TO MY LOU
(WITH ALTERNATING-THUMB ROLL)

Track 13 🔊

G

Strings:	3	2	5	1	4	2	5	1		3	2	5	1	4	2	5	1
Right hand:	T	I	T	M	T	I	T	M		T	I	T	M	T	I	T	M
Count:	1	+	2	+	3	+	4	+		1	+	2	+	3	+	4	+
Lyrics:	Skip,				skip					skip		to	my	Lou.			

D7

3	2	5	1	4	2	5	1		3	2	5	1	4	2	5	1
T	I	T	M	T	I	T	M		T	I	T	M	T	I	T	M
1	+	2	+	3	+	4	+		1	+	2	+	3	+	4	+
Skip,				skip					skip		to	my	Lou.			

G

3	2	5	1	4	2	5	1		3	2	5	1	4	2	5	1
T	I	T	M	T	I	T	M		T	I	T	M	T	I	T	M
1	+	2	+	3	+	4	+		1	+	2	+	3	+	4	+
Skip,				skip					skip		to	my	Lou.			

D7 ... **G**

3	2	5	1	4	2	5	1		3	2	5	1	4	2	5	1
T	I	T	M	T	I	T	M		T	I	T	M	T	I	T	M
1	+	2	+	3	+	4	+		1	+	2	+	3	+	4	+
Skip,		to	my	Lou		my			dar	-			ling.			

TIP
Almost all beginners have trouble changing chords while maintaining a steady roll pattern in the right hand. You should already be comfortable fretting the chords you need to play in a song before adding roll patterns. When playing with others or with the audio, let the right hand lead the left. It's more important to keep playing in rhythm when playing with others. Your left hand will catch up with more practice.

Tablature, or TAB for short, is a visual way to show the music that is played on the banjo. TAB uses some elements of standard musical notation and other elements that are unique to the banjo. Tablature is like standard music notation in that it indicates what notes to play. In addition, it also tells you which strings to play, what right-hand fingers you'll use, and whether the string you play is fretted or open. If a string is to be fretted, TAB also indicates where on the neck you'll fret with the left hand.

The five horizontal lines represent the banjo strings, with the first string on the top line and the fifth string on the bottom line. This is similar to the way the strings appear when you look down at them while playing.

Measures (or bars) mark off musical time and are separated by barlines, as you have already seen. Each measure contains one cycle of four beats (called quarter notes), equal to one roll pattern of eight eighth notes.

Eighth notes in tablature are indicated by a vertical line called a stem and a horizontal beam that connects one note to another. Every measure must be filled up with music, silence, or a combination of both that equals the amount of time taken up by our even count of eight notes (or "1 & 2 & 3 & 4 &"). This is called "four-four" time, and is shown by the time signature $\frac{4}{4}$ at the beginning of each tune. It means that there are four beats in every measure (represented by the top "4") and that a quarter note (represented by the bottom "4") gets one beat.

Here's how the alternating-thumb rolls for the G, C, and D7 chords appear in tablature, demonstrated on **Track 14**. For the G chord, all of the numbers are 0s because this chord is unfretted. For the C and D7 chords, the numbers 1 and 2 match the fretted positions used for these chords. A metronome introduces the tempo with four clicks and the progression is played twice. Here, you'll play two roll notes (eighth notes) for every click (quarter note) of the metronome.

Track 14

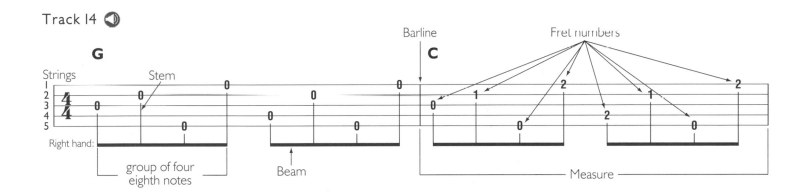

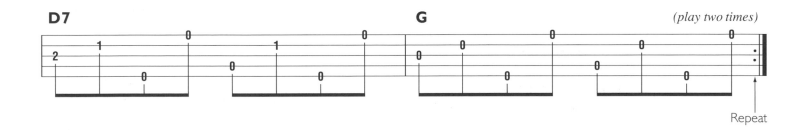

The Forward-Backward Roll

Let's try a new roll. Like the alternating-thumb roll, the forward-backward roll is also made up of eight notes. This roll is a natural one for the right hand.

We'll try it first with the G chord, demonstrated on **Track 15** . Play this roll over and over again until you can hit the correct notes most of the time without any effort at all.

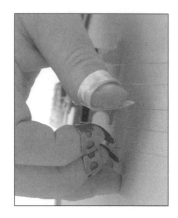 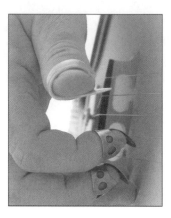  

Strings:	3	2	1	5
Right hand:	T	I	M	T
Count:	1	+	2	+

 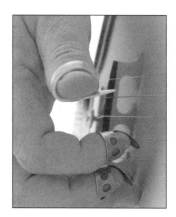 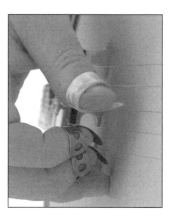 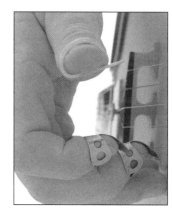

Strings:	1	2	3	1
Right hand:	M	I	T	M
Count:	3	+	4	+

Now try playing this roll over the G, C, and D7 chords in succession, demonstrated on **Track 16** . You'll hear four clicks from the metronome to give you the tempo.

Once again, you'll play two roll notes for every click of the metronome. Try to go from one chord to the next without stopping the flow of notes in the right hand.

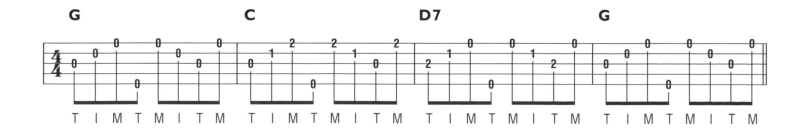

G   C   D7   G

T I M T M I T M T I M T M I T M T I M T M I T M T I M T M I T M

Now let's play this roll as an accompaniment to "Man of Constant Sorrow." You've already learned how to strum and change chords to this song. The chord progression for this tune is four measures of G, two measures of C, two measures of D7, and two measures of G. The forward-backward roll fills exactly one measure of time. To play this roll as an accompaniment to the song, play the forward-backward roll four times with the G chord, two times with the C chord, two times with the D7 chord, and two times with the G chord.

Track 17 demonstrates the forward-backward roll for two verses of "Man of Constant Sorrow." When you are able to play this new roll slowly and change chords without stopping, try playing along with the audio track. The chord progression shown here is played four times on the recording and you'll be playing two roll notes for each click of the metronome.

MAN OF CONSTANT SORROW
(WITH FORWARD-BACKWARD ROLL)

Track 17

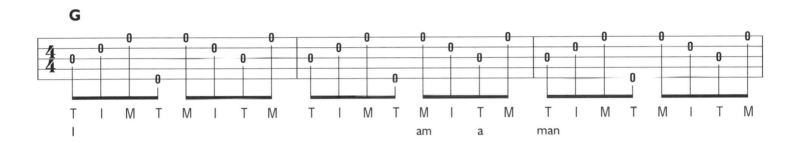

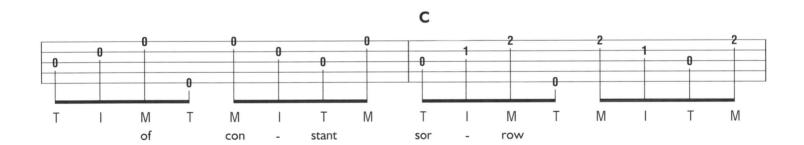

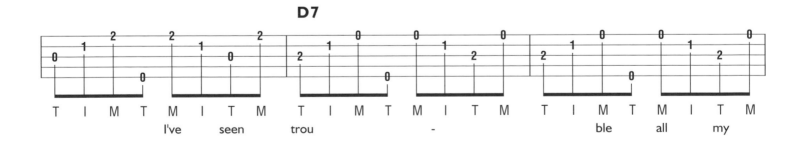

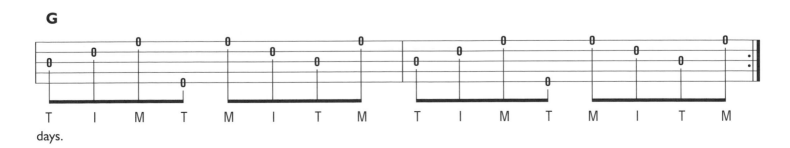

Now let's return to "Will the Circle Be Unbroken" and "Long Journey Home" and try using the alternating-thumb roll and the forward-backward roll to accompany each song.

Let's first review the chord progressions:

Will the Circle Be Unbroken
4 measures of G / 2 measures of C / 7 measures of G /
1 measure of D7 / 2 measures of G

Long Journey Home
6 measures of G / 1 measure of C / 6 measures of G /
1 measure of D7 / 2 measures of G

This time around, let's dispense with the TAB and use our ears to follow the chord progressions. First, try an alternating-thumb roll for both tunes. Then, once you're comfortable with this roll, try the forward-backward roll.

Because each roll has eight notes, they are interchangeable with one another when used to accompany a song.

Listen to **Track 18** to hear "Will the Circle Be Unbroken" with an alternating-thumb roll and **Track 19** for "Long Journey Home" with the alternating-thumb roll. **Track 20** demonstrates "Circle" with a forward-backward roll and **Track 21** shows "Long Journey Home" with the forward-backward roll. You'll hear a count-in for each tune to give you the correct tempo. Play two eighth notes for each quarter-note click of the metronome.

Once you are comfortable using both roll patterns as an accompaniment to these songs, you can try using both rolls together in the same song. Try playing the alternating-thumb roll followed by the forward-backward roll for the G, C, and D7 chords to get used to this new technique.

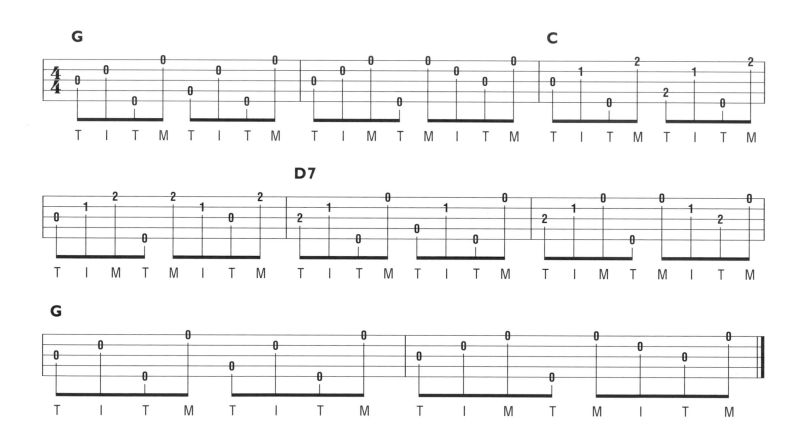

Track 22 demonstrates the sound of using the alternating-thumb and forward-backward rolls one after the other for the G, C, D7, and G chords.

Track 23 demonstrates "Will the Circle Be Unbroken?" using the alternating-thumb and forward-backward rolls.

Track 24 demonstrates these rolls for "Long Journey Home."

TIP
It's a good idea to learn the chord shapes on the guitar for the chords that you play on the banjo. You can then more quickly learn a new chord progression when playing with others by following the chords played by the guitar player.

The *pinch pattern* is another frequently used right-hand banjo technique. The pinch pattern fills up an entire measure just like a roll pattern, but this time only four notes are played instead of eight.

With this technique, each note lasts twice as long as the notes played in a roll pattern. Because of this, the notes that make up the pinch pattern are called *quarter notes*. One quarter note takes up the rhythmic space of two eighth notes, or one quarter of a measure of $\frac{4}{4}$ time.

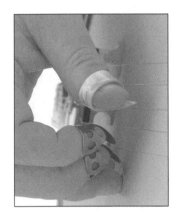 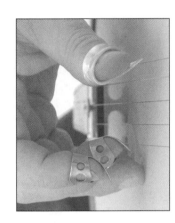  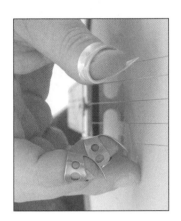

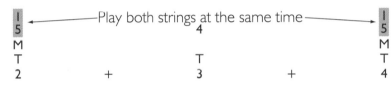

Strings:	3		1 5 M	Play both strings at the same time 4		1 5 M
Right hand:	T		T	T		T
Count:	1	+	2	+ 3	+	4 +

In tablature, a quarter note is indicated by a stem coming down from the note, but there are no beams attaching quarter notes together as there are with eighth notes. Another unique aspect of the pinch pattern is that you will play more than one string at the same time.

This is indicated in the tablature with these notes positioned on top of one another vertically. Here is the pinch pattern in tablature for the G, C, and D7 chords (demonstrated on **Track 25**):

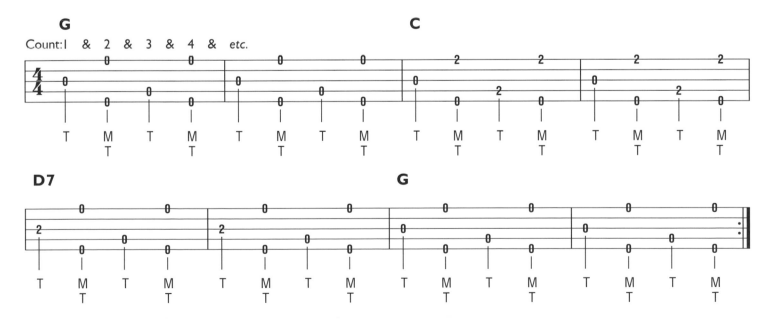

Now try using the pinch pattern for the four songs you've learned so far. You've already learned the chord progressions to these tunes and played these songs with the alternating-thumb and forward-backward rolls.

This time around, substitute the pinch pattern for the roll patterns and change chords as before. You'll be playing half as many notes with the pinch pattern because these notes are quarter notes and last twice as long.

Mixing Rolls and the Pinch Pattern

Track 26 🔊 demonstrates the pinch pattern for "Skip to My Lou"

Track 27 🔊 demonstrates the pinch pattern for "Man of Constant Sorrow"

Track 28 🔊 demonstrates the pinch pattern for "Will the Circle Be Unbroken?"

Track 29 🔊 demonstrates the pinch pattern for "Long Journey Home"

I bet you've already guessed what's next! Let's now try playing roll patterns and the pinch pattern together in "Skip to My Lou."

Remember that the notes of the pinch pattern will last twice as long as the notes in the alternating-thumb roll. **Track 30** 🔊 demonstrates "Skip to My Lou" using the alternating-thumb roll and pinch pattern.

SKIP TO MY LOU
(ALTERNATING-THUMB ROLL AND PINCH)

Track 30 🔊

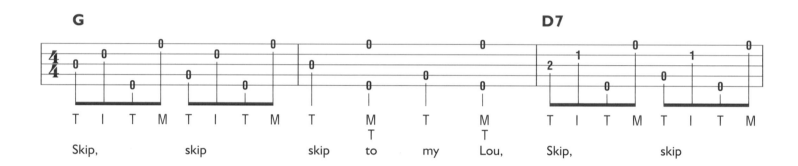

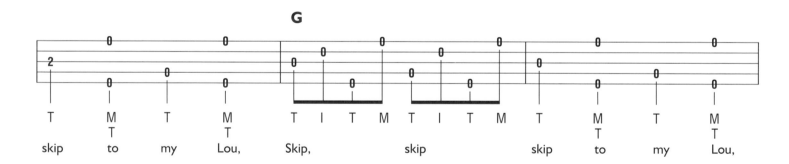

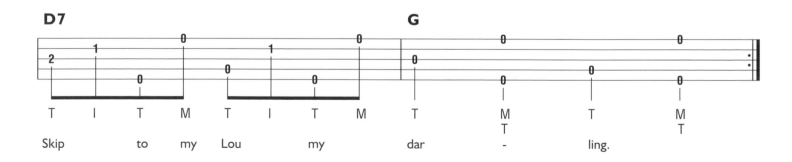

Now try this with the forward-backward roll and the pinch pattern, demonstrated on **Track 31** .

SKIP TO MY LOU
(FORWARD-BACKWARD ROLL AND PINCH)

Track 31

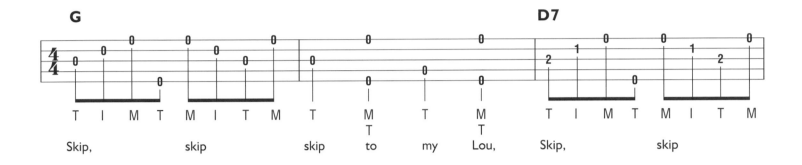

Skip, skip skip to my Lou, Skip, skip

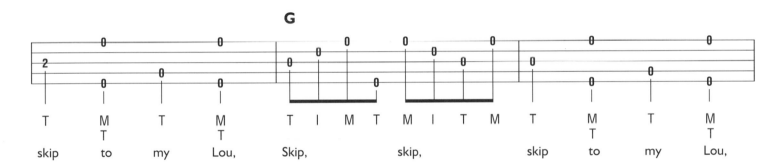

skip to my Lou, Skip, skip, skip to my Lou,

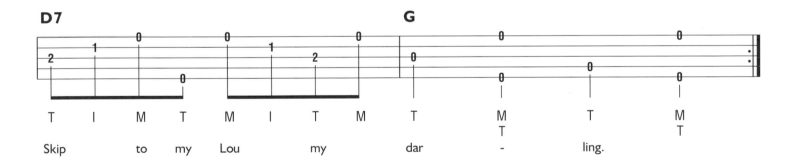

Skip to my Lou my dar - ling.

TIP

It's important to keep a steady beat going now that you are playing notes of different rhythmic values. Some players keep this beat going in their head, matching their internal sense of the beat to what their hands are playing. Other musicians like to tap their foot to help establish the beat or practice with a metronome that supplies the beat.

Finding the Melody

Your banjo playing will be much more interesting and exciting when you add melody notes to the right-hand patterns that you've learned. Below is an easy version of the melody to "Skip to My Lou." Notice that there are several notes in this melody that don't have either a stem or a flag attached to them.

These are *half notes* and they last twice as long as quarter notes and four times as long as eighth notes. **Track 32** demonstrates the melody for "Skip to My Lou." **Track 33** demonstrates the same melody with band accompaniment (played twice).

SKIP TO MY LOU
(EASY MELODY)

Track 32 & Track 33

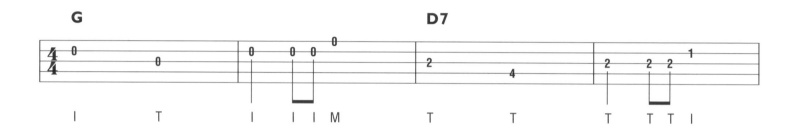

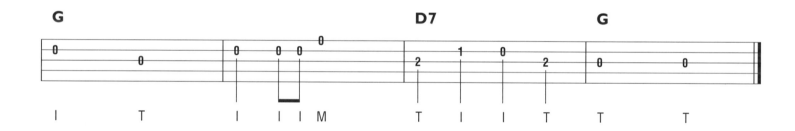

This melody sounds a bit sparse all by itself. Fortunately, we have plenty of musical space to add some of the right-hand ideas we've been practicing. Let's now try a banjo solo to "Skip to My Lou," using the alternating-thumb roll and pinches.

We'll use two different kinds of D7 chords in this version. For the first measure of D7, your left-hand index finger will fret the third string at the second fret and your ring finger will fret the fourth string at the fourth fret. For the second measure of D7, shift back to the more familiar fretted position.

D7 (new)

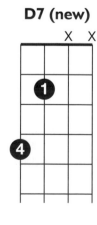

D7

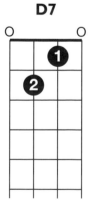

Track 34 🔊 demonstrates the banjo solo for "Skip to My Lou" using the alternating-thumb roll and pinches.

Track 35 🔊 demonstrates this solo at a faster tempo with band accompaniment (played twice).

SKIP TO MY LOU
(SOLO 1)

Track 34 🔊 & Track 35 🔊

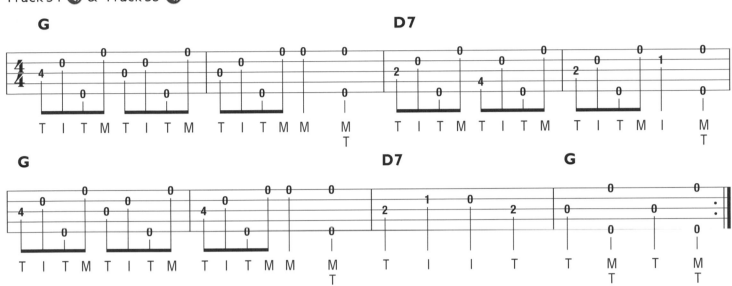

Here's another solo to "Skip to My Lou." This time we'll use the forward-backward roll and pinches. **Track 36** 🔊 demonstrates this banjo solo using the forward-backward roll and pinches.

Track 37 🔊 demonstrates this solo at a faster tempo with band accompaniment (played three times).

SKIP TO MY LOU
(SOLO 2)

Track 36 🔊 & Track 37 🔊

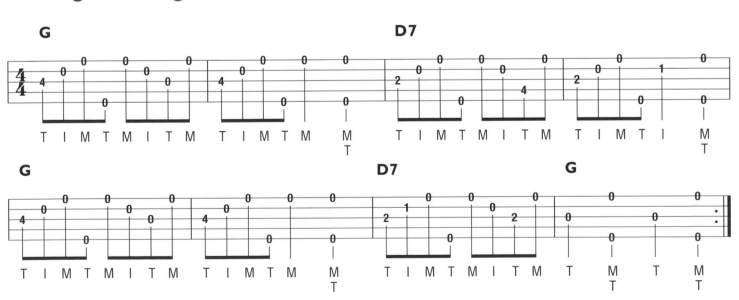

Which one sounds best to you? The first version captures the melody more precisely while the second version seems to flow more smoothly.

They are different from one another but they both work. This is one of the great things about bluegrass banjo. Even experienced players remain fascinated with the many ways to work up a banjo solo.

Let's Play with the Band!

It's time to show your stuff! The next four tracks on the audio feature our great backup band without the banjo. With each song, try using the combinations of roll and pinch patterns that are the most comfortable to play and that sound best to you.

Try to use as many combinations as you can—there is no one "correct" way to accompany these songs. Focus on keeping in rhythm with the rest of the band and not stopping the flow of notes in your right hand.

Track 38 🔊 SKIP TO MY LOU
Track 39 🔊 MAN OF CONSTANT SORROW
Track 40 🔊 WILL THE CIRCLE BE UNBROKEN?
Track 41 🔊 LONG JOURNEY HOME

Cripple Creek—The international banjo anthem!

No banjo instruction book would be complete without presenting a version of one of the most popular banjo songs in the world, "Cripple Creek." As you learn new techniques in the future, feel free to update this basic version. Each line is repeated once in "Cripple Creek." This repetition is shown in the tablature by *repeat signs,* the two vertical lines and dots that enclose the area to be repeated.

Track 42 🔊 demonstrates the "Cripple Creek" solo shown below, and Track 43 🔊 demonstrates this solo played through three times with the band at a faster tempo. Track 44 🔊 provides the back-up band for your own banjo solo!

CRIPPLE CREEK

Track 42 🔊 , Track 43 🔊 & Track 44 🔊

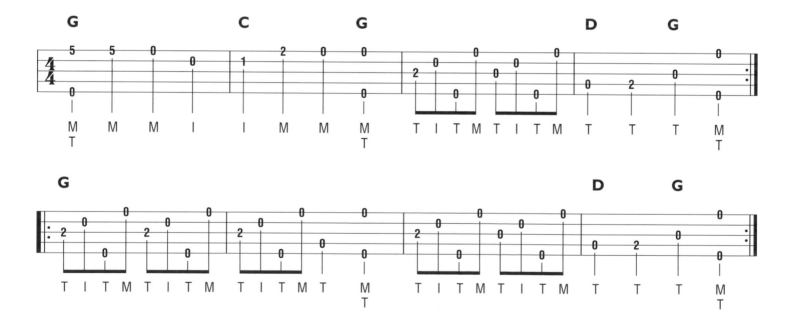

Chord Diagrams—Recap

A *chord diagram* is a widely used method to express which fingers and frets are used to play banjo chords. If you turn the banjo around with the neck facing you, you'll see how the banjo neck is represented in a chord diagram.

The vertical lines represent the banjo strings, with the leftmost line being the fourth string and the rightmost line being the first string. Since it is fretted infrequently, the fifth string is usually not shown in a chord diagram. The thick horizontal line at the top represents the nut. The second line from the top is the first fret and the line below is the second fret. Circles indicate which strings are fretted and at what fret. The numbers inside the circles tell you which fingers are used at each position.

In this chord dictionary you will find several versions of each chord using different arrangements of the notes (also called *voicings*). These chords can be substituted in any of the songs in this book. Once you have learned the chords, go back to the songs and experiment.

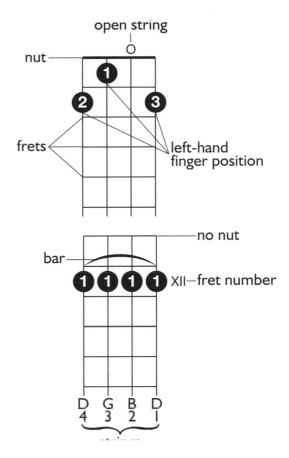

G
Open

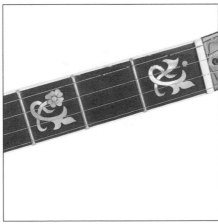

G

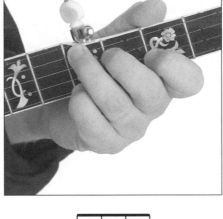

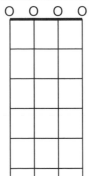

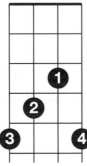

G

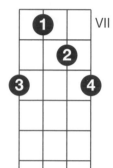

VII

G

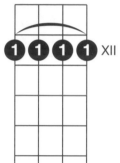

XII

G

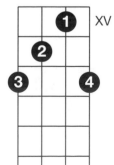

XV

C

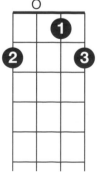

O

C

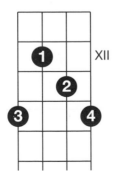

C

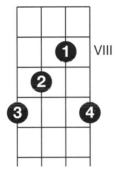

VIII

C

XII

D7

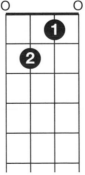

D

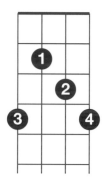

D

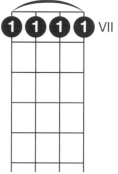

VII

D

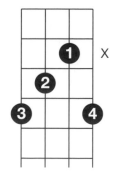

X

D

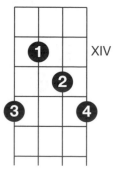

XIV

I hope that you've enjoyed playing the songs in this book. I also hope that you're excited about learning even more about bluegrass banjo. Now that you've mastered these basic techniques you have a solid foundation for successfully playing music with others as well as tackling more advanced playing. You're now ready to proceed to the next step on your musical journey.

Today, it's never been easier to learn how to play. There are many good books and instructional videos available on the market for you to explore and you might even want to attend a banjo instructional camp for a total immersion experience.

Chances are good that there is a banjo teacher, a jam session, a festival or a bluegrass concert series close to where you live. Seek out the advice of the folks at your regional acoustic music store to get more involved in your local scene. The more exposure you have to other banjo players and bluegrass musicians, the more quickly you'll learn and the more enjoyment you'll get back.

Good luck and keep on picking!

Bill Evans

Additional Lyrics

Long Journey Home

Black smoke arising and it surely is a train.
Surely is a train boys, surely is a train.
Black smoke arising and it surely is a train.
I'm on my long journey home.

My baby left me, she's gone away,
She's gone away, boys, she's gone away.
My baby left me, she's gone away,
I'm on my long journey home.

I'm leaving on the evening train, count the days I'm gone,
Count the days I'm gone, boys, count the days I'm gone.
I'm leaving on the evening train, count the days I'm gone,
I'm on my long journey home.

Chorus:
Lost all my money but a two-dollar bill,
Two-dollar bill boys, a two-dollar bill.
Lost all my money but a two-dollar bill and
I'm on my long journey home.

Man of Constant Sorrow

I am a man of constant sorrow,
I've seen trouble all my days.
I bid farewell to old Kentucky,
The place where I was born and raised.

For six long years I've been in trouble,
No pleasure here on earth I find.
For in this world I'm bound to ramble,
I have no friends to help me now.

It's fare thee well my own true lover,
I never expect to see you again.
For I'm bound to ride that northern railroad,
Perhaps I'll die upon this train.

You can bury me in some deep valley,
For many years where I may lay.
Then you may learn to love another,
While I am sleeping in my grave.

It's fare you well to a native country,
The places I have loved so well.
For I have seen all kinds of trouble,
In this cruel world, no tongue can tell.

Maybe your friends think I'm just a stranger,
My face you'll never see no more.
But there is one promise that is given,
I'll meet you on God's golden shore.

Skip To My Lou

Flies in the buttermilk, shoo, fly, shoo.
Flies in the buttermilk, shoo, fly, shoo.
Flies in the buttermilk, shoo, fly, shoo.
Skip to my lou, my darling.

Chorus:
Skip, skip, skip to my Lou.
Skip, skip, skip to my Lou.
Skip, skip, skip to my Lou.
Skip to my Lou my darling.

Will the Circle Be Unbroken?

I was standing by my window
On a cold and cloudy day,
When I saw that hearse come rollin'
For to carry my mother away.

Lord, I told the undertaker,
"Undertaker, please drive slow,
For this body you are hauling,
Lord, I hate to see her go."

Oh, I followed close behind her,
Tried to hold up and be brave,
But I could not hide my sorrow
When they laid her in the grave.

Chorus:
Will the circle be unbroken,
By and by, Lord, by and by?
There's a better home awaiting
In the sky, Lord, in the sky.

San Francisco Bay Area resident **Bill Evans** is known worldwide for being both a superb bluegrass banjo player and a master teacher. Bill is a popular instructional columnist for *Banjo Newsletter* magazine and hosts his own banjo camp each year with Sonny Osborne in the Nashville, Tennessee area. He also hosts two popular instructional AcuTab Publications DVDs, *Up The Neck Backup For Bluegrass Banjo* and *Playing Banjo Backup in a Bluegrass Band*. He has recorded two critically acclaimed banjo CDs, *Native and Fine* (Rounder) and *Bill Evans Plays Banjo* (Mighty Fine Records), and has taught courses in American music at San Francisco State University, the University of Virginia, and Duke University. He currently tours with his solo historical show "The Banjo in America." To learn more about Bill, visit www.nativeandfine.com

Suggested Listening

Tom Adams
Right Hand Man (Rounder CD-0282)

Alison Brown
Stolen Moments (Compass 4400)

J. D. Crowe with The Bluegrass Album Band
The Bluegrass Compact Disc (Rounder CD-11502)

Charlie Cushman
Five String Time (County CMC-001)

Bill Evans
Native & Fine (Rounder 295)
Bill Evans Plays Banjo (Mighty Fine Records 906)

Lester Flatt and Earl Scruggs
Foggy Mountain Banjo (County 100)

Belá Fleck
The Bluegrass Sessions: Tales From The Acoustic Planet, Vol. 2
  (Warner Brothers 47332)

Bill Keith
Something Auld, Something Newgrass, Something Borrowed,
  Something Bluegrass (Rounder 84)

Jim Mills
Hide Head Blues (Sugar Hill 4004)

Alan Munde
Festival Favorites Revisited (Rounder 311)

The Osborne Brothers
The Bluegrass Collection (CMH 9011)

Earl Scruggs
The Essential Earl Scruggs (Columbia CD 90858)

Sammy Shelor
Leading Roll (Sugar Hill 3865)

Ralph Stanley and the Clinch Mountain Boys
Classic Bluegrass (Rebel 1109)

Tony Trischka
World Turning (Rounder 294)

Pete Wernick
On A Roll (Sugar Hill SH-CD-3815)

Also from the Music Sales
Banjo Collection

The Banjo Picker's Fakebook
By David Brody

The ultimate sourcebook for banjo players! Contains over 230 jigs, reels, rags, hornpipes, and breakdowns from all major traditional instrumental styles. Includes discography and special introductory materials on regional styles, interpretation and bluegrass techniques.

HL14003289

The Banjo Player's Songbook
By Tim Jumper

Arranged for the five-string banjo in easy-to-play tablature, every style of music is represented in this giant volume of over 200 songs. Includes lyrics to folk songs, sentimental favorites, holiday songs, sing-alongs, and more!

HL14003285

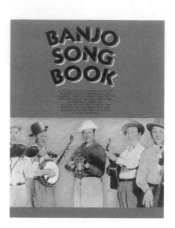

Banjo Song Book
By Tony Trischka

A thorough survey of the three-finger picking classics of the early 1900s, transitional styles of the 1930s, the Scruggs style of the 1940s, and beyond! There are instructional sections on Scruggs, Reno, and melodic picking, plus more than 75 tunes in tablature.

HL14003286

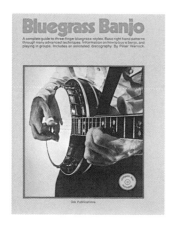

Bluegrass Banjo
By Peter Wernick

Thirty-five songs offering a complete exploration of bluegrass music. Includes music theory, tips on performance, bluegrass ensemble playing, back-up playing, and a wealth of banjo lore. Features "Oh Susannah," "Skip To My Lou," and more! For beginners and advanced players.

HL14004651

Melodic Banjo
By Tony Trischka

A complete instruction guide to "Keith style" banjo technique. Over 30 tunes and songs by Bill Keith, Eric Weissberg, Alan Munde, Bobby Thompson, Vic Jordan, and others. Contains descriptions of their personal playing styles as well as interviews.

HL14021162

Banjo Case Chord Book
By Larry Sandberg

Find the banjo chords you need instantly! This handy manual is conveniently sized at 4.5 by 12 inches, allowing you to take it everywhere. The book includes many fingerings for each chord, charts for using chords in any key, a complete tuning chart, and more!

HL14024235